Original title:
The Arctic Moose

Author: Sabrina Sarvik
ISBN HARDBACK: 978-9908-1-0004-3
ISBN PAPERBACK: 978-9908-1-0005-0
ISBN EBOOK: 978-9908-1-0006-7

Guardians of the Snowy Expanse

Under the glittering skies so bright,
The guardians dance, a joyous sight.
With laughter ringing, spirits soar,
In the snowy expanse, forevermore.

Snowflakes twirl like dreams in flight,
Warmth abounds in the crisp, cold night.
Children build with laughter loud,
In the purity of the shimmering shroud.

Majesty in White

Veils of white on hills so grand,
Nature's artwork, a gentle hand.
Festive hearts in gardens wake,
As winter's splendor, the world will take.

The sunbeams dance on ice so clear,
Whispers of joy bring loved ones near.
In every corner, cheer ignites,
Embracing warmth on frosty nights.

Shadows of the Icebound Forest

Among the trees where shadows play,
Festive echoes guide the way.
Twinkling lights on branches sway,
In the icebound forest, night turns day.

A wooden sleigh dashes through the pines,
Laughter weaves through snowy thines.
Whispers of magic fill the air,
As winter's charm draws us to share.

Wilderness Wanderer

Through snow-kissed trails the wanderer roams,
A festive spirit in nature's homes.
With every step, the world feels new,
The wilderness sings in vibrant hue.

Joyful echoes of hearts in flight,
Under stars that sparkle bright.
Adventure waits in the falling snow,
As the wanderer embraces the glow.

Frosty Ambassadors

Snowflakes dance on twinkling lights,
Laughter echoes through the nights.
Children's joy in every cheer,
Frosty ambassadors draw us near.

Hot cocoa warms our frozen hands,
Candy canes in winter's lands.
Together we celebrate the dream,
In this festive, twinkling gleam.

Harmony in a Frozen Landscape

Whispers of winter fill the air,
Nature's canvas, pure and rare.
Unfurling wonders wrapped in white,
Harmony sings with pure delight.

Icicles hanging in the glow,
Silent symphonies in the snow.
Every flake tells a story shared,
A frozen landscape, magic declared.

Silent Giants of the Woodlands

Majestic trees in snowy crowns,
Silent giants wear white gowns.
Branches sway with gentle grace,
In winter's hold, a warm embrace.

As stars above begin to gleam,
Nature hums a joyful dream.
With each step in the soft white,
We celebrate the magic night.

Tracks in the Silent Snow

Footprints mark our joyful path,
In the snow, we share a laugh.
Each step leads to wonders new,
Tracks in white, a festive hue.

As we wander, hearts aglow,
Embracing all the charm of snow.
In tranquil woods, we weave our song,
Tracks in the silent snow belong.

Shadows in White

In the glow of lanterns bright,
Laughter dances in the night,
Children's voices fill the air,
Joy is found everywhere.

Snowflakes twirl like gentle dreams,
Wrapped in warmth, together it seems,
Festive spirits rise and flow,
Hearts aglow with winter's show.

Chiming bells from town to town,
Gifts we share, no hint of frown,
Merry feasts and friends abound,
Magic lives where love is found.

Underneath the shining stars,
Wishes whispered, near and far,
In the night so crisp and clear,
We gather close, we hold what's dear.

Emperors of the Wintry Realm

Amidst the frost, we constellate,
Majestic figures, celebrate,
Cloaked in snow, we claim our reign,
In this kingdom, joy is gained.

Radiant lights from every tree,
We dance in puresynd, wild and free,
Underneath the northern sky,
Emperors brave, we dwell on high.

From the hearth, warm stories weave,
In every heart, we believe,
Candies sweet and laughter loud,
Embracing warmth in every crowd.

As dawn approaches, chill recedes,
We plant our dreams like tiny seeds,
Knowing well, through frost and flame,
Our wintry joy will stay the same.

Guardians of the Snowy Hollow

In the hollow, soft and bright,
Guardians dance in pure delight,
With every footstep, winter smiles,
Warming souls across the miles.

Echoes of laughter blend with cheer,
Filling hearts with holiday spirit here,
In snowflakes' touch, we find our place,
Embracing all with gentle grace.

With every spark from evening's fire,
Our hopes and dreams reach higher and higher,
We share our tales beneath the stars,
United under winter's bars.

Snowy paths lead tales anew,
For every friend, a bond so true,
In the hollow, together we stand,
Guardians of joy, hand in hand.

The Call of the Icy Pathways

Hear the call of icy ways,
Whispers drift in frosty haze,
With every step, the world shines bright,
Journey forth into the night.

Through glistening trees, we weave our tale,
Where laughter rings, and spirits sail,
Brightened faces, joy unveiled,
The heart of winter, never failed.

With snowflakes swirling on the breeze,
We gather close, hearts find their ease,
Celebrations across the land,
Together, united, we take a stand.

In each frosty breath, we find the cheer,
The pathways echo with love so near,
As festive tunes drift through the air,
The call of winter, beyond compare.

Majestic Shadows in Pale Light

In the glow of the pale moon's beam,
Shadows dance, a delightful dream.
Joyous laughter fills the night air,
Whispers of magic linger there.

Starry breezes twirl through the trees,
Bringing whispers carried by the freeze.
Colors burst from lanterns so bright,
Embracing hearts in this festive light.

Guardian of the Snowy Expanse

Amidst the snow that sparkles and gleams,
The guardian watches over sweet dreams.
Children's laughter echoes so clear,
As joyous spirits draw ever near.

Footprints trace tales where magic is spun,
In frosty realms where the day's almost done.
A celebration held, both grand and bright,
In the heart of winter's blissful night.

Glacial Grace Beneath Northern Skies

Under the canvas of twinkling stars,
Glacial wonders whisper from afar.
Every breath brings the crispness of cheer,
As joyful moments gather near.

The auroras dance overhead like fire,
Painting the night with a wild desire.
A feeling of wonder, pure and so rare,
Wraps every soul in this shimmering air.

Starlit Solitude of the Wilds

In the solitude where the wild things roam,
Stars guide the way as shadows find home.
Nature's orchestra plays a sweet song,
In harmony, where we all belong.

Campfires flicker with tales from the past,
Memories gathered, some fleeting, some vast.
A gathering of spirits beneath the night sky,
Forging connections that never say goodbye.

Reflections in Icy Waters

The sun reflects on frozen lakes,
Children laugh, the joy awakes.
Colors dancing, bright and bold,
Stories whispered, dreams unfold.

Skates glide softly, winter's grace,
Chasing shadows, we embrace.
Echoes of laughter fill the air,
Moments cherished, beyond compare.

Frostbitten Footprints

Footprints leave a tale behind,
Impressions soft, the heart aligned.
Snowflakes glitter, pure and white,
Guiding paths to pure delight.

With every step, the whispers play,
In frosty fields, we dance and sway.
Joyful spirits, wild and free,
In winter's arms, we feel the glee.

Serenade of the Silent Plains

Beneath the stars, the plains awake,
A melody, the night shall make.
Whispers float on frosty breeze,
Echoing sweetly through the trees.

In this hush, our laughter sings,
Joyful hearts, with love it brings.
Together under moonlit skies,
Where every dream and wish flies.

A Dance in the Snowfall

Glistening flakes begin to swirl,
In the magic, we twirl and whirl.
A dance of joy on winter's stage,
Moments captured, hearts engage.

Laughter rises, spirits soar,
Echoing through the festive lore.
In the snowfall, dreams ignite,
A tapestry of pure delight.

Serene Majesty in Frigid Climes

In frosty air, the laughter rings,
Beneath the glow, the wild heart sings.
Snowflakes twirl like dancers bright,
Each step a spark, pure and light.

The world adorned in crystal lace,
Joyful faces, a warm embrace.
Whispers of joy in the frozen night,
Serenade the stars, a twinkling sight.

Echoes of cheer on winter's breeze,
Happiest hearts swaying with ease.
Amidst the cold, we gather near,
Embracing the warmth, spreading cheer!

With each soft step, let comfort grow,
In serene majesty, the love we show.
In frigid climes, our spirits rise,
A fest of dreams beneath cold skies.

The Beauty in the Chill

The winter's breath a crisp delight,
Each flake a star in frosty night.
Children's laughter fills the air,
Joy unbounded, beyond compare.

Trees in white, a fairytale scene,
Shimmers dance, a world so clean.
In the chill, the fires glow,
Hearts grow warmer, love in tow.

Candles flicker, casting gold,
Stories cherished, timeless and bold.
Underneath the moon's soft gaze,
We weave our dreams in a smoky haze.

The beauty found in winter's chill,
Soft whispers in the night, we thrill.
Together we bask in love's embrace,
A festive journey, a shared grace!

Aurora's Dance with the Giants

In the sky, the colors roam,
As auroras dance, they find their home.
Giants of ice, they stand so tall,
Witness the spectacle, a wondrous call.

Whirling lights, a vibrant show,
Painting whispers on the snow.
Nature's canvas, splashed with flair,
A celebration in frigid air.

Amid the frosty, glimmering night,
Hearts ignite with pure delight.
Together we sway, beneath the beams,
Lost in the magic, we weave our dreams.

Each breath we take is a melody sweet,
In joyous reverie, our hearts meet.
Aurora's dance, a celestial chance,
In the chill, we all find romance!

Legends Carved in Ice

Carved in ice, the tales unfold,
Of ancient spirits, brave and bold.
Each shard a whisper from days gone by,
Festive echoes beneath the sky.

Underneath the blankets of white,
Legends shimmer, bringing delight.
Stories shared by the fireside glow,
Binding our hearts as our laughter flows.

In the stillness, we gather here,
Tales of wonder, joy, and cheer.
With every laugh, the past ignites,
Painting moments that feel so bright.

In ice and snow, our dreams take flight,
In simple joys, our spirits ignite.
Legends carved in the festive air,
Together forever, our hearts laid bare.

Frosted Dreams Await

In fields of white, the laughter flows,
With twinkling lights, the evening glows.
We gather round, so warm and bright,
As dreams take flight on this wondrous night.

The stars above, a sparkling show,
With every heart, the joys will grow.
A dance through snowflakes, a winter's jest,
In frosted dreams, we find our rest.

Dance of the Midnight Sun

Beneath the sky, the colors swirl,
As laughter rises, hearts unfurl.
The midnight sun begins to gleam,
In joyous rhythm, we chase the dream.

With every step, the shadows play,
In warm embrace, we greet the day.
A tapestry of love and grace,
In vibrant hues, we find our place.

Rugged Majesty

On mountain peaks where eagles soar,
The call of nature, forevermore.
With every step on this rugged land,
The spirit dances, wild and grand.

The whispers of the ancient trees,
Bring forth the tales upon the breeze.
In rugged beauty, we stand tall,
Together, we embrace it all.

Echoes of the Frozen Wilderness

In silence deep, the snowflakes fall,
Revealing secrets, nature's call.
With every breath, the crisp air sings,
Of winter's wonders and hidden things.

The frozen lake, a mirror bright,
Reflects the joy of pure delight.
In wild expanse, where dreams take flight,
Echoes linger through the night.

Boundless Horizons

Bright balloons dance in the sky,
Laughter rings as friends draw nigh.
With colors bold, hearts are free,
Boundless joy for all to see.

Swaying gently, the leaves hum,
A sweet tune that bids us come.
Under the sun's warm embrace,
We celebrate in this joyous space.

Candles flicker, the stars ignite,
Sharing stories deep into night.
Under a vast, endless dome,
In each other, we find our home.

With glasses raised, we toast today,
To love and laughter, come what may.
In this moment, nothing's amiss,
We revel in our boundless bliss.

Solitude Amongst the Pines

Whispers of wind through the trees,
Nature sings soft melodies.
Underneath the sprawling boughs,
In peace, the heart quietly vows.

Snowflakes twirl like cotton dreams,
Moonlight glistens on silver streams.
A fire crackles, warm and bright,
As shadows dance in winter's light.

The world beyond fades away,
In solitude, I choose to stay.
Amongst the pines, my spirit soars,
In nature's arms, my heart restores.

With every breath, a moment to keep,
In tranquil silence, I gently seep.
Festive whispers in the night,
In solitude, I find my light.

Monarch of the Winter Solstice

Crowned with light, the night wears gold,
Legends of yore, beautifully told.
Frosty air and twinkling stars,
Joyful hearts, no care for scars.

Gathered round, we share a cheer,
With laughter bright, the end draws near.
Cookies baked, and cocoa warm,
In this season, we're all reborn.

Nature whispers in the chill,
A promise to our hearts to fill.
For every moment, a chance to embrace,
In this festival, we all find grace.

As shadows lengthen, spirits rise,
Under the magic of winter skies.
With every flicker, hope takes flight,
In the solstice glow, we unite.

To the monarch of this festive night,
We pledge our love, and bask in light.
Hand in hand, we sing our tune,
Together, we dance beneath the moon.

Crossover into the Arctic Realm

Glistening ice and a sky so blue,
Adventurers gather, a vibrant crew.
With sleds and sled dogs, we race along,
Celebrating life with a joyous song.

The northern lights paint the starry night,
Dancing waves of color, pure delight.
With every breath, the cool air sings,
In this arctic world, the spirit springs.

Festive fires blaze, stories ignite,
Youthful laughter pierces the night.
In every glance, a shared embrace,
Together, we cherish this precious space.

The chill around brings us near,
In the kingdom of snow, we shed our fear.
With hopes as bright as the sky's grand dome,
In this arctic realm, we find our home.

Beneath the Moonlit Blanket

Beneath the moonlit blanket, we dance,
The stars above twinkle in a trance.
Laughter echoes through the night,
As fireflies join in pure delight.

With cheerful hearts, we sing our songs,
In joyful steps, where each belongs.
The world is bright, our spirits soar,
Together we celebrate, wanting more.

Candles flicker with a golden hue,
While the breeze whispers secrets anew.
Hands held tight, we twirl and spin,
In this festive moment, we all win.

So raise a glass, let joy ignite,
Beneath the moonlit blanket tonight.
In every smile, and glance we share,
A bond grows strong, beyond compare.

Chronicles of the Snowbound Monarchs

In winter's grasp, the monarchs meet,
Among the icy halls, their reign is sweet.
With crowns of frost and cloaks of white,
They gather 'round, in pure delight.

The air is crisp, with laughter bright,
As stories flow under the starlit night.
Each tale spins dreams of realms afar,
While snowflakes twirl like wishes in a jar.

Holidays warm with a regal cheer,
A banquet spread, their friends draw near.
With every toast of hearty cheer,
The bonds of kinship grow sincere.

Let music play, let spirits gleam,
In snowbound halls, where hopes redeem.
A festive tale of joy and mirth,
In chronicles woven on this earth.

Frosty Legends of a Forgotten Realm

In frosty legends, stories unfold,
Of brave souls' journeys, daring and bold.
Through ancient woods where shadows creep,
The heart of winter holds secrets deep.

A festive fire warms the chilled air,
As we gather round, with friends to share.
Each whispered tale brings smiles to light,
While snowflakes swirl, a magical sight.

The whimsical creatures dance in delight,
As frost-kissed dreams take airy flight.
With laughter ringing, the night grows bright,
Forgotten realms revive, shining white.

So take our hands, let's spin and glide,
Through frosty legends, side by side.
In every moment, let joy be revealed,
In the warmth of friendship, hearts are healed.

The Resilient Drift

In the drifting snow, we find our way,
With steadfast hearts, we greet the day.
From icy trails, our spirits rise,
In the blanket of white, we touch the skies.

With every step, resilience grows,
Through swirling winds and winter's throes.
Together we stand, in a snowy trance,
As hope unfolds in a jubilant dance.

The laughter of children fills the air,
In snowball fights and joyful flair.
A sledding race down hills so steep,
In moments like these, our hearts do leap.

So let us cherish this frosty drift,
In unity, through every rift.
In the radiant glow of season's cheer,
We find our strength, year after year.

An Ode to the Frost-Kissed Giant

In winter's embrace, a giant stands tall,
Beneath a blanket of shimmering white.
With branches adorned in crystal and sprawl,
He whispers to stars through the long, frosty night.

Children gather 'round, laughter fills the air,
Hot cocoa held tight in small, eager hands.
They dance like the snowflakes, a beautiful pair,
While dreams of warm summers slip like fine sands.

Joy spreads like light in the crisp, morning glow,
Each twinkle a promise of warmth just ahead.
The frost-kissed giant, so gentle, will know,
That spring will awaken, but now, let's be fed.

With carols of joy, the night settles deep,
While memories shimmer like stars on the way.
An ode to this giant, our hearts, he will keep,
In the festival glow of our cold holiday.

Veil of the Northern Mystique

Under the shroud of a midnight sky,
The northern lights dance with an ethereal grace.
Whispers of magic linger nearby,
In the chill of the air, we gather in place.

A fire crackles, casting gold on the night,
With stories exchanged that echo with cheer.
Hearts beat together in warmth, pure delight,
As we savor the moment, the season draws near.

The snowflakes fall soft as the music surrounds,
A melody wrapped in the hush of the calm.
In the atmosphere, festive life resounds,
Each note is a gift, a delightful balm.

Hands raised in warmth, we toast to the skies,
To family and friends, and the dreams that we weave.
In the veil of the night, our laughter still flies,
Creating a tapestry we seldom believe.

Lullabies of the Cold Moon

Beneath the soft beam of a cold, silver moon,
A hush blankets all, wrapped in silence so sweet.
Snowflakes perform like a soft, gentle tune,
Singing lullabies to the world at our feet.

The stars twinkle brightly in frosty delight,
Guiding lost wanderers back home to their dreams.
The night calls us close, holding magic in sight,
As laughter and warmth weave enchanted themes.

Cups clink with joy, merry voices arise,
Echoing stories of moments held dear.
The moon takes its watch, gracing night's deepest sighs,
Cradling us all in its glow, soft and clear.

In the stillness, we pause, hearts drumming with cheer,
For the magic of winter brings us ever near.
Lullabies of love drift on icy cold air,
Awakening spirits, igniting our flare.

Heartbeat Beneath the Snow

Underneath layers of soft, glistening white,
The heartbeat of nature still stirs and beats on.
With whispers of life that come back into light,
As winter's embrace continues till dawn.

Children craft stories in snow with delight,
Building their dreams in fortresses tall.
Giggles and laughter rise up in the night,
While stars overhead bear witness to all.

The warmth of our hearth, a beacon so bright,
Calls out to the hearts wrapped in cold winter's breath.
We gather together, encompassed in light,
Finding joy in each moment, defying all death.

Heartbeat beneath snow, life pulses anew,
With each falling flake, a tale yet untold.
In the dance of the frost, we'll always renew,
For the festival spirit in winter's strong hold.

Frosted Antlers Under Starry Skies

In the glow of twilight's cheer,
Antlers frosted, shining clear.
Laughter dances in the air,
Joyful whispers everywhere.

Beneath the stars, we gather round,
In the silence, love is found.
Warm cocoa, fireside bright,
Embracing magic of the night.

Snowflakes twirl, a festive sway,
Twinkling lights, they lead the way.
Hearts aglow, our spirits high,
Underneath this vast, wide sky.

Let the music fill the night,
Voices blending, pure delight.
Frosted antlers, stars above,
We celebrate, share our love.

A Lullaby for Winter Giants

Whispers soft as snowflakes fall,
Winter giants stand so tall.
In their shadows, dreams awake,
Lullabies the wise ones make.

Underneath a quilt of white,
In the calm of frosty night.
Stars above, a shining guide,
Joyful hearts, with love abide.

Breezes sing a gentle tune,
While the earth sleeps 'neath the moon.
Warming wishes on the breeze,
Bringing peace, hearts at ease.

Fires crackle, stories shared,
In this moment, none compared.
A lullaby for all to hear,
Winter giants, we hold dear.

Solitary Sentinels

Trees stand guard in soft white cloaks,
Solitary sentinels, wise oaks.
Branches cradling the falling snow,
Holding secrets from long ago.

In twilight's embrace, they appear,
Whispers of wonders echo near.
Dancing shadows in the light,
Creating magic through the night.

Winter's breath runs cool and deep,
While the world around us sleeps.
Sentinels, so tall and proud,
Guarding dreams within the shroud.

In their presence, time stands still,
Heartbeats echo, calm and thrill.
Solitary, yet not alone,
In their arms, we've found a home.

Beneath the Glimmering Ice

Crystal surfaces, bright and clear,
Beneath the glimmering ice, we cheer.
Children laughing, spirits soar,
Together we find joy once more.

Skates glide smooth on frozen trails,
As winter's magic gently prevails.
Each twirl, a story, graceful flight,
Underneath the shimmering light.

Carols sung by fireside glow,
Memories linger, soft and slow.
Beneath the ice, a world alive,
In our hearts, traditions thrive.

Gathered close, with warmth to share,
Love surrounds in winter's air.
Beneath the glimmering ice, we find,
The joy of life, forever entwined.

Vibrance Against the Whiteback

Colors erupt in a frosty scene,
Joyful laughter, a bounding spark,
Warmth and cheer, a radiant sheen,
Life anew, igniting the dark.

Snowflakes dance in a swirling flight,
A festive cheer, the world aglow,
Brightly wrapped gifts, a pure delight,
In every heart, the joy does grow.

Carolers sing 'neath the twinkling stars,
Voices blend in harmonious tunes,
With every note, sorrows are far,
Magic weaves 'neath the glowing moons.

Together we raise our mugs with glee,
To friendship forged in the winter's breath,
In vibrant moments, hearts are free,
Celebration dances, alive, not death.

Woodland Titan's Lament

In the hush of a snow-clad wood,
A titan stands with branches bare,
Whispers lost where the wild once stood,
Yet festive spirits float in the air.

Tales of old in the crisp, cold night,
Fires aglow with stories spun bright,
Nature sighs under starry sight,
Echoing joy in the soft twilight.

Underneath a canopy of snow,
Life breathes deep, though the world lies still,
Laughter's echo makes the shadows glow,
Every moment cherished, heart to fill.

A dance of the leaves on a brisk wind,
Whispers of warmth 'neath the frozen sigh,
In this woodland, our stories blend,
Together we dream as the moments fly.

Cries of the Chilled Wilderness

In the depths of the forest, spirits cry,
Echoes of joy beneath icy trails,
As laughter rings 'neath the moonlit sky,
The heart awakens, winter exhales.

Snow-draped pines with a glistening crown,
Whispers of wonder on every breath,
Festive joys never let us down,
In this embrace of life and death.

Gather 'round for a tale so bold,
Where warmth and mirth forever dwell,
In the chill, there's a story told,
A tapestry woven, weaves its spell.

The wilderness thrums with a vibrant beat,
A symphony composed of pure delight,
Hands intertwined, feeling the heat,
Together we rise, hearts shining bright.

Silence of the Frozen Whispers

In silence wrapped, the world resigned,
A frozen hush blankets the ground,
Yet festivity hums, joy defined,
In every corner, warmth is found.

Snowflakes flutter on a gentle breeze,
Timid whispers of the coming cheer,
Echoes of laughter, an open seize,
In the heart of winter, love draws near.

Candles flicker on the windowsill,
Glistening softly against the night,
With every glow, the cold we kill,
The silence breaks with our shared delight.

In this stillness, spirits take flight,
Each breath a promise, bright and true,
Together we dance in the moonlight,
With frozen whispers, we start anew.

Silent Splendor of the Chilling North

Snowflakes twirl in the evening light,
Candles flicker, hearts so bright.
Laughter echoes through the air,
Joyous spirits everywhere.

Icicles shimmer like diamonds near,
Warmth and cheer hold us dear.
The world dressed in winter's attire,
Fires burn with a joyful fire.

Carolers sing by the shimmering tree,
Voices blend in sweet harmony.
Bells ring out, a festive tune,
Celebrating under the glowing moon.

Antlers Against the Aurora

Amidst the pines, a flickering dance,
Under the auroras, we take a chance.
Antlers crowned in frost and light,
We gather close on this magical night.

Stars above in a violet glow,
Whispers of midnight breezes blow.
With each step, we leave a trace,
Legends born in nature's grace.

Together we share stories old,
In warm embrace against the cold.
Festive hearts like the skies above,
United in laughter, peace, and love.

Frosted Hooves on Icy Trails

Hooves crunch softly on the frozen ground,
Echoes of joy in the silence abound.
Each stride we take in this crisp delight,
Paints our journey with pure starlight.

The air is sweet with pine and cheer,
Every breath brings the season here.
Snowflakes fall, like whispers glide,
In nature's embrace, we take pride.

Sleigh bells jingle in the night,
Creating magic, pure and bright.
With loved ones close, we share our song,
In this wonderland where we belong.

Whispers of the Frozen Tundra

The tundra sleeps beneath a quilt,
Of icy dreams and warmth built.
Stars twinkle in the vast expanse,
Inviting all to join the dance.

Frosty winds carry tales so grand,
Of joy and laughter across the land.
From every corner, voices rise,
A celebration beneath the skies.

Brightly lit, the world aglow,
As kindred spirits come to show.
In the frozen air, our hearts entwine,
Festive souls in perfect line.

Celestial Antlers in Twilight

As dusk descends in golden light,
The deer with antlers, a stunning sight.
Twinkling stars in the velvet sky,
Whispers of magic as night draws nigh.

Beneath the glow of the moon's embrace,
Nature dons a festive face.
Joyful echoes of laughter soar,
In this wonderland, we explore.

With every step on the frosted ground,
A melody of winter's sound.
Celebrations dance in the cool night air,
A tapestry woven with beauty rare.

Let candles flicker and fires burn bright,
In the heart of this chilly night.
Together we sing, together we cheer,
Under celestial antlers, we're all here.

Shadows Long on Snowy Plains

In the stillness of the frosty morn,
Shadows stretch where dreams are born.
Snowflakes twirl like festive sprites,
Painting the world with shimmering whites.

Children laugh as they race and glide,
Snowball fights in the hillsides wide.
Warm cocoa shared by the crackling fire,
Amidst the chill, hearts never tire.

Each footprint whispers tales of joy,
Of winter's magic, a treasured toy.
As nature dons her sparkling gown,
We find our joy in this snowy town.

Beneath the sky, so vast and blue,
Every moment feels fresh and new.
In snowy plains where shadows play,
We celebrate life in a grand array.

Frosty Dreams of a Winter Wanderer

Through the woods, a wanderer roams,
In frosty dreams, he finds his homes.
Whispers of winter, tales unfold,
Of ancient legends, brave and bold.

Each flake that falls, a story spun,
Under the gaze of the winter sun.
With every breath, a plume of steam,
He weaves his journey, a frosty dream.

Candles flicker in cozy nooks,
By the firelight, there are tales in books.
Songs of old fill the winter night,
With laughter and joy, everything feels right.

As he wanders through snow-laden trees,
The chill in the air sings soft melodies.
In frosty dreams, where wonder thrives,
He finds the magic that truly arrives.

Underneath the Boreal Canopy

Underneath the boreal trees,
Soft whispers echo in the breeze.
Icicles glisten like crystal charms,
Winter's embrace, a world in arms.

Friends gather 'round for warmth and cheer,
Festive spirits fill the atmosphere.
Laughter dances on the frosty air,
In this enchanted, wintry lair.

The fire crackles, stories unfold,
Of wandering hearts, both young and old.
Snow blankets the earth in a soft embrace,
Amidst the joy, we find our place.

Underneath stars that twinkle bright,
We celebrate life on this magical night.
Embracing the beauty, let our hearts sing,
Underneath the canopy, we find our spring.

Elegy for a Hoofed Monarch

In fields where shadows dance and play,
The hoofed monarch roams by day.
With regal stride and gentle grace,
He wanders through this lively place.

With laughter ringing in the air,
The flowers bloom without a care.
His steps create a joyful beat,
In nature's rhythm, pure and sweet.

But whispers float like autumn leaves,
Reminders of what time bereaves.
Yet in this moment, spirits rise,
In festive songs beneath the skies.

So raise a glass to nights so bright,
To hoofed kings under soft moonlight.
We celebrate, we laugh, we sing,
In memory of our cherished king.

Glacial Grace

In shimmering fields of ice and snow,
Where winter winds gracefully blow.
Dancing lights in the frosty air,
Echo laughter without a care.

The world adorned in crystal white,
A festive scene, a pure delight.
Together we gather, warm and near,
Sharing tales, spreading cheer.

Icicles hang like chandelier lights,
Reflecting dreams on glittering nights.
With every moment, joy entwined,
In glacial realms, our hearts aligned.

So let us toast to winter's glow,
A celebration of life in tow.
Embracing cold with hearts ablaze,
In this magical, glacial grace.

Fur-Trimmed Giants

Beneath the canopy of vibrant trees,
Fur-trimmed giants sway with the breeze.
Adorned in colors, bright and bold,
A festive tale of nature told.

Their laughter roars, a joyful sound,
As they dance upon the fertile ground.
Leaves like confetti fill the air,
With every step, they banish care.

Gathered together, spirits entwined,
In this summer warmth, we find.
Magic woven in every glance,
Inviting us to join the dance.

So let's embrace this vibrant scene,
And celebrate where we have been.
In fur-trimmed wonders, hearts unite,
In fields alive with pure delight.

Echoes of the Boreal Realm

In the whispering woods where shadows play,
Echoes of laughter fill the day.
With pines standing tall, dressed in green,
A festival of life, a vibrant scene.

The air is brisk, the spirit's free,
In every moment, there's jubilee.
Birdsong flutters like ribbons bright,
A melody that ignites the night.

With friends beside us, we share a feast,
In nature's bounty, our joy increased.
Around the fire, stories weave,
In the boreal glow, we believe.

So let us honor this wild embrace,
In echoes of joy, we find our place.
In the realm where dreams are born,
We celebrate anew each morn.

Heartbeat of the Far North

Drums of joy echo far and wide,
Under stars, we dance with pride.
Colors swirl in joyous glee,
Celebrate together, you and me.

Snowflakes twirl, a dazzling sight,
Twinkling lights shine through the night.
Voices raise in spirited song,
In the heart of winter, we belong.

Families gather, laughter soars,
Wrapped in warmth, our hearts explore.
Fires crackle, stories unfold,
In this magic, our dreams are bold.

With each heartbeat, the night ignites,
In the Far North, our spirits take flight.
Together we bask in this embrace,
A festive echo, a joyful space.

Twilight in the Frost

Twilight drapes a silver shawl,
Frosty whispers, a gentle call.
Candles flicker, shadows play,
In this moment, we sway and stay.

Sipping cocoa, warm and sweet,
Friends around, the night's complete.
Laughter dances, filling the air,
Every heart knows joy is rare.

Snowflakes glisten like diamonds bright,
Under the soft and shimmering light.
Twilight magic envelops us whole,
Filling each heart, warming each soul.

In silence, we cherish, we dream,
The frosty night, a gentle theme.
Together we stand, hand in hand,
In the twilight, a festive land.

Beneath the Endless Sky

Beneath the endless sky we cheer,
Fires ablaze, our hearts sincere.
Starry wonders twinkle above,
In the chill, we feel the love.

Gatherings bright, with smiles so wide,
Under the stars, side by side.
Songs of joy rise with the moon,
A melody sweet, a festive tune.

Chill in the air, warmth all around,
In laughter's echo, our joy is found.
With every star, a wish is made,
In the night, our fears do fade.

Together we share this magical night,
Beneath the sky, everything feels right.
Unity sparkles in every eye,
In this festive moment, we reach for the sky.

Throne of Frost and Snow

Upon the throne of frost and snow,
We gather together, our spirits aglow.
In winter's grasp, our hearts align,
With every laugh, our souls entwine.

Hot cider brews, aromas rise,
Underneath winter's painted skies.
With every cheer, we share our dreams,
In this wonderland, everything gleams.

Snowflakes fall, a soft embrace,
Creating memories, time can't erase.
In each twirl and festive dance,
We seize the night, we take a chance.

Royal joy in each heartbeat flows,
On the throne of frost, our friendship grows.
For in the cold, our warmth is true,
In this festive throne, it's me and you.

Glistening Gait of the Winter Sentinel

In the hush of snowflakes that swirl and dive,
The sentinel dances, keeping dreams alive.
Each footfall whispers, a crystal embrace,
Painting the world with a silver lace.

Under the moon's watch, the shadows play,
Lights twinkle gently, guiding the way.
Joy paints the night with laughter and song,
In this frosty realm, we all belong.

Elves in the pines, they weave cheer so bright,
Gathering warmth in the cloak of night.
With every twirl of the winter's delight,
Hearts beat together, a festive sight.

Glistening breath of the sentinel's cheer,
Bringing the friends we hold oh so near.
Together we stand, beneath starlit skies,
In the dance of the winter, our spirits will rise.

Dance of the Polar Dawn

As daylight awakens on icy terrain,
The colors of morning begin to remain.
Ribbons of red and gold fill the air,
A tapestry woven, beyond compare.

Hushed whispers echo through trees draped in white,
The dawn greets the world, with a dazzling sight.
Laughter erupts, as the children take flight,
In the dance of the dawn, hearts feel so light.

Snowflakes like jewels, they shimmer and spin,
With each joyful leap, let the festivities begin.
Across the vast lands, a jubilant sound,
As cheers intertwine, with warmth all around.

Embrace the magic, let worries away,
Dance through the morning, bask in the play.
In the glow of the dawn, our spirits unite,
A celebration of life, in pure delight.

Majesty in a Frozen Realm

Piercing the silence, a melody so grand,
Majestic creations adorn winter's hand.
Icicles hanging like crystal chandeliers,
Whispering secrets throughout the years.

Families gather, their smiles aglow,
In the heart of the realm, the warm fires flow.
Stories retold, with shimmers of light,
In this frozen kingdom, warmth feels just right.

Golden laughter dances on shimmering snow,
While hearts flutter freely, embraced by the glow.
The night sparkles softly, as if it could sing,
In the majesty found, as the season takes wing.

A chorus of voices, in harmony rise,
In this wondrous winter, the spirit flies.
With every shared moment, the joy makes its claim,
In the frozen realm, we all feel the same.

The Tremor of Silent Steps

Beneath the dark sky, with stars shining bright,
The tremors of footsteps bring warmth to the night.
Each crunch on the snow brings laughter so near,
A symphony woven, for all to hear.

Gathering 'round, as friends hold their breathe,
In silence we walk, facing winter's depth.
The night whispers secrets, inviting us close,
In the still of the air, we find what we chose.

With candles aglow, the path lights the way,
Flickering flames dance as children will play.
In shadows that shift, we find our own cheer,
In the tremor of steps, the happiness here.

Ode to the moments we cherish and keep,
With laughter and stories, our memories leap.
In this night of wonder, where joy takes its stance,
The tremor of silent steps leads us to dance.

Gentle Monarch of the Boreal

In the canopy above, whispers sing,
Dancing leaves catch the joy of spring.
Gentle monarch, breathing light,
The forest alive, in colors bright.

Snowflakes swirl in a playful race,
Softly landing, a delicate lace.
Under the stars, laughter sways,
In the grip of winter's holiday.

Fires crackle, warmth ignites,
Voices blend like the night's delights.
Joyful hearts gather near,
In the embrace of festive cheer.

As dawn unfolds, the colors bloom,
Nature's canvas, dispelling gloom.
The gentle monarch leads the way,
In the boreal kingdom, we dance and play.

Untamed Spirit of the Glacial Wild

Winds howl fierce through icy halls,
Yet beneath, a wild spirit calls.
With laughter stacked on frozen peaks,
Adventure breathes, the heart it seeks.

Glaciers glisten, a dazzling sight,
While the sun sets, painting the night.
Wildness flows in each snow-clad ridge,
Nature's festival, our own great bridge.

Beneath the stars, stories unfold,
Warm drinks and camaraderie bold.
The spirit soars, untamed and free,
In the glacial wild, we revel with glee.

Each whisper of snow, a song in the air,
Echoes of joy, everywhere.
In icy realms, we find our thread,
Untamed spirit, where dreams are fed.

Resilience in the Arctic Stillness

Amidst the quiet of the frost,
Resilience blooms, never lost.
Silent strength in the snow's embrace,
Life persists, at its own pace.

Icicles hang like chandeliers,
Reflecting warmth through frozen years.
In every nook where shadows play,
Hope ignites, chasing gray away.

With each step on the crunching ground,
In solitude, sweet joy is found.
Through chill and silence, spirits blend,
A festive heart, on nature depend.

The Northern Lights swirl in delight,
Painting dreams across the night.
In stillness, we sing, we strive,
Resilience thrives, forever alive.

The Solitary Path of the North

A path unfolds through endless white,
Each breath a story in the night.
Footprints dance on a crystal sea,
The solitary way, alive and free.

Harsh winds whisper ancient tales,
Of spirits that glide on northern trails.
A lantern glows, warmth from within,
Guiding the heart where joy begins.

As shadows drift and laughter soars,
In every echo, adventure roars.
Moments gleam like stars above,
A festive spirit, wrapped in love.

The solitary path leads us home,
Through wild terrains where we roam.
Under the auroras, we take our stand,
Together as one, hand in hand.

Embrace of the Winter Woods

The trees adorned in sparkling white,
Whispers of joy fill the frosty air.
Snowflakes dance in the silver light,
Nature's beauty, beyond compare.

Children laughing, traces in snow,
Creating memories, moments so bright.
In the woods where warm feelings flow,
Hearts aglow with pure delight.

Fires crackle, warmth draws near,
Hot cocoa steaming, friendships bloom.
In the embrace, we shed our fear,
Wrapped in love, dispelling gloom.

Evening stars twinkle high above,
A canvas painted with dreams anew.
In winter's heart, we find our love,
Together, always, me and you.

Chronicles of the Snow-Capped Wanderer

A wanderer strides through silent drifts,
Footsteps whisper tales untold.
In the hush, the spirit lifts,
Glimmers of magic, brave and bold.

Mountains rise, their peaks aglow,
Clad in ivory, a regal dress.
Each trail reveals where dreams can flow,
With every step, we seek success.

Crisp air tinged with pine's embrace,
Nature's perfume, pure and clean.
Wanderer's heart quickens its pace,
In awe of sights that must be seen.

At dusk the sky a painting bright,
As colors blend in twilight's grace.
Snow-capped wonders steal the night,
In every corner, a warm embrace.

Serenity in a World of White

A blanket drapes the earth in peace,
Silence whispers secrets soft and low.
In this purity, worries cease,
A tranquil moment in white's glow.

Each branch, each flake, a work of art,
Nature's canvas, crafted with care.
In winter's grasp, we feel the heart,
Of serenity, fluttering in the air.

Footprints venture on paths untraced,
Curiosity leads us to explore.
Within this world, time is embraced,
As joy and laughter open the door.

Fireside tales shared with delight,
Radiance warms the gathering crowd.
In this sanctuary, hearts take flight,
A world of white, cherished and proud.

Echoes Among the Flurries

Flurries twirl in playful cheer,
Dancing lightly with winds that play.
In this wonder, joy draws near,
Every moment, a bright bouquet.

Voices mingle, laughter rings,
Children dash 'neath a flurry of white.
In the frosty air, happiness sings,
As winter weaves its magic light.

Snowmen rise with a silly grin,
Scarves of color, hats askew.
In these moments, our hearts begin,
To cherish all that we hold true.

Evening falls with a shimmering glow,
Stars emerge in the velvet blue.
In echoes soft, our love will grow,
Amid the flurries, me and you.

Heart of Ice in the Realm of Giants

In lands where shadows dance and play,
The giants roam beneath stars' sway.
With icy breath, they greet the night,
Their hearts ablaze with festive light.

The crystal trees in laughter sway,
As snowflakes twirl in bright array.
Adventure calls with joyous cheer,
In this grand realm, there's naught to fear.

With every step, the ground does shine,
A festive spirit intertwines.
In giant hearts, warmth starts to rise,
Amidst the cold, the warmth belies.

So let us join in joyful song,
Embrace the night where we belong.
In realms of ice and spirits bright,
We'll celebrate this wondrous sight.

Grace Beneath the Northern Lights

Under the glow of emerald skies,
A dance unfolds where silence lies.
Each flicker brings a tale untold,
Of grace and joy that won't grow old.

The snowflakes pirouette with glee,
In patterns only hearts can see.
With laughter spilled across the night,
We gather round the shimmering light.

With every breeze, a story flows,
In whispered tones the spirit grows.
The northern lights, our guiding grace,
As we, united, find our place.

So hand in hand, beneath the glow,
We'll celebrate the warmth we know.
In every twinkle, joy ignites,
Together here, beneath the lights.

Whispers of the Frozen Tundra

In the tundra's vast, enchanted land,
Whispers echo, soft and grand.
The quiet night is filled with cheer,
As festive magic draws us near.

Crystals glimmer in the pale moonlight,
A celebration of winter's might.
With each hushed word, the stories flow,
Of wonder lost in ice and snow.

The twilight sparkles, spirits soar,
As laughter echoes forevermore.
With friends beside, we celebrate,
The moments shared, however late.

So listen close to the wind's sweet sigh,
As the frosty breath of joy goes by.
In this frozen realm, our hearts take flight,
In whispers soft, our dreams ignite.

Antlers Beneath the Northern Lights

Beneath the glow of dancing stars,
The antlers rise as if from Mars.
In festive joy, they touch the sky,
With stories woven, spirits fly.

Amongst the snow, a gathering grows,
With laughter deep, and warmth that glows.
The northern lights, a vibrant hue,
A tapestry of red and blue.

We share our dreams, each gentle glance,
As swirling winds invite the dance.
Together here, we find our way,
In harmony, we're led to play.

So let us raise our voices high,
In nature's choir, we will not shy.
With hearts that beat to festive rhymes,
Beneath the lights, we stand through time.

Tales of Ice and Shadows

In the glimmer of frostbite glow,
Laughter rings through the air,
Children dance on shimmering snow,
Dreams twirl without a care.

Candles flicker in windows bright,
Whispers of joy, warmth, and cheer,
Stars twinkle on a crisp, clear night,
As friends gather near and dear.

Tales of old resound and play,
Around the fire's glowing heart,
Magic wraps us in its sway,
As shadows and light depart.

Memories woven like a quilt,
Under the vast, starry sky,
With every story, warmth is built,
As time gently drifts and sighs.

Frost's Embrace

Frosted branches, silver and white,
Glisten under the moon's soft kiss,
Crisp air sings of pure delight,
A world awash in frosty bliss.

Skaters glide on the frozen lake,
Joyful cheers break the starry night,
With every turn, our spirits wake,
An embrace of winter's light.

Bonfire crackles, embers soar,
As tales take flight on swirling smoke,
We gather closer, yearn for more,
In this warmth, our laughter broke.

Every whispered word, a bond,
In the chill, we find our place,
In winter's grasp, our hearts respond,
With love and joy we interlace.

Awakenings in the Chill

Awake to the shimmer of dawn's first light,
Frost flowers bloom where the shadows lay,
Every flake dances, a glittering sight,
As the world greets a brand new day.

Delightful aromas waft through the air,
Cinnamon spices and cocoa warm,
Joyful gatherings, laughter to share,
In every heart, a spark to charm.

Snowflakes swirl, a silent ballet,
Whispers of wonder beneath the sky,
In winter's grasp, our spirits play,
As seasons change, we sigh and fly.

With every heartbeat, stories unfold,
In chilly embraces, we come alive,
In frost-kissed moments, memories gold,
Our festive spirits continue to thrive.

Whispering Winds on Icebound Shores

Whispers of winds through icy trees,
Call to the souls who seek and roam,
Frost-kissed breezes bring forth the keys,
To the hearts that yearn for home.

Waves lap softly on shores adorned,
With crystal gems of frosty sheen,
In every gust, a spirit warmed,
A promise held in the unseen.

The fire flickers as stories flow,
Of distant lands and winter dreams,
In this embrace, we come to know,
We're woven tight in laughter's seams.

As dusk settles, stars brightly gleam,
In the chill, we find our light,
Amidst the shadows, hopes redeem,
With festive hearts, we ignite the night.

Crystalline Majesty

Sparkling snowflakes dance and twirl,
Glistening under the sun's warm glow.
Children laugh with joy, unfurled,
Winter magic puts on a show.

Lit trees shimmer in the night,
Bells chime as hearts start to soar.
Each moment a pure delight,
Gathered friends at the door.

Cider warms the chilly breeze,
Joyous songs fill the air with cheer.
Frosted branches sway with ease,
Together we hold loved ones near.

As stars wink, the night takes flight,
In crystalline glory, we stand tall.
Such beauty fills our hearts with light,
In this season, we feel it all.

Sentinel of the Thawing Dawn

The sun rises gently over the hill,
Whispering secrets of warmth and grace.
Nature stirs from its winter chill,
Awakening dreams in a soft embrace.

Colors bloom, a radiant display,
Birds chirp sweetly, a welcoming song.
Life returns in a glorious way,
A celebration where all belong.

Glistening rivers warmly flow,
Melting ice reveals hidden trails.
Laughter echoes, a vibrant glow,
In this moment, the spirit prevails.

With each sunrise, new joys appear,
Nature's canvas painted bright and bold.
Together we thrive, singing clear,
In the thawing dawn, stories unfold.

Wanderer's Watch

Beneath the stars, in quiet delight,
A wanderer gazes, the world so vast.
Each twinkle a beacon, guiding the night,
With dreams unfurling, shadows cast.

Moonlit paths call gently near,
As whispers of adventure unfold.
The chill of the breeze, a thrill to hear,
With hopes aglow, a heart turns bold.

Footsteps crunch on crisp, frosty ground,
Fires flicker in the distance, bright.
In this evening's embrace, joy is found,
A tapestry woven of warmth and light.

Wanderer's watch, under the sky,
Navigating life, a dulcet song.
Each star a reminder to soar and fly,
In this festive journey, we all belong.

Harmony of Frost and Form

In winter's embrace, the world is still,
Frost-kissed branches weave a soft lace.
Nature's beauty, a testament of will,
In this moment, we find our place.

Taste the sweetness of gingerbread cakes,
The scent of pine fills the air around.
With every laugh, the heart awakens,
In harmony, joy can be found.

Candles flicker with a warm, soft glow,
Stories shared by the fireside's heat.
As the season's magic starts to flow,
Unity makes our hearts skip a beat.

Together we stand, hand in hand,
Celebrating life in this festive form.
In winter's embrace, we understand,
With love and joy, we weather the storm.